Out of the Dark ol' Midnite

A Poetic Journey in Four Acts

by
cj fletcher

Out of the Dark ol' Midnite

A Poetic Journey in Four Acts

by cj fletcher

Out of the Dark ol' Midnite

By cj fletcher

First Edition

Author: cj fletcher
Editor: Paul Gilliland
Formatting: Southern Arizona Press
All Artwork: Canvi

Published by Southern Arizona Press
Sierra Vista, Arizona 85635
www.SouthernArizonaPress.com

ISBN: 978-1-960038-12-0

Poetry

Preface

The Dark Ol' MidNite resides in us all. It is up to each of us to find the way out. cj fletcher has pursued music, art, poetry, writing, religion, and various high-risk endeavors in an effort to free himself. The Jury, shall we say, is still out on the matter.......

Contents

The Journey   36

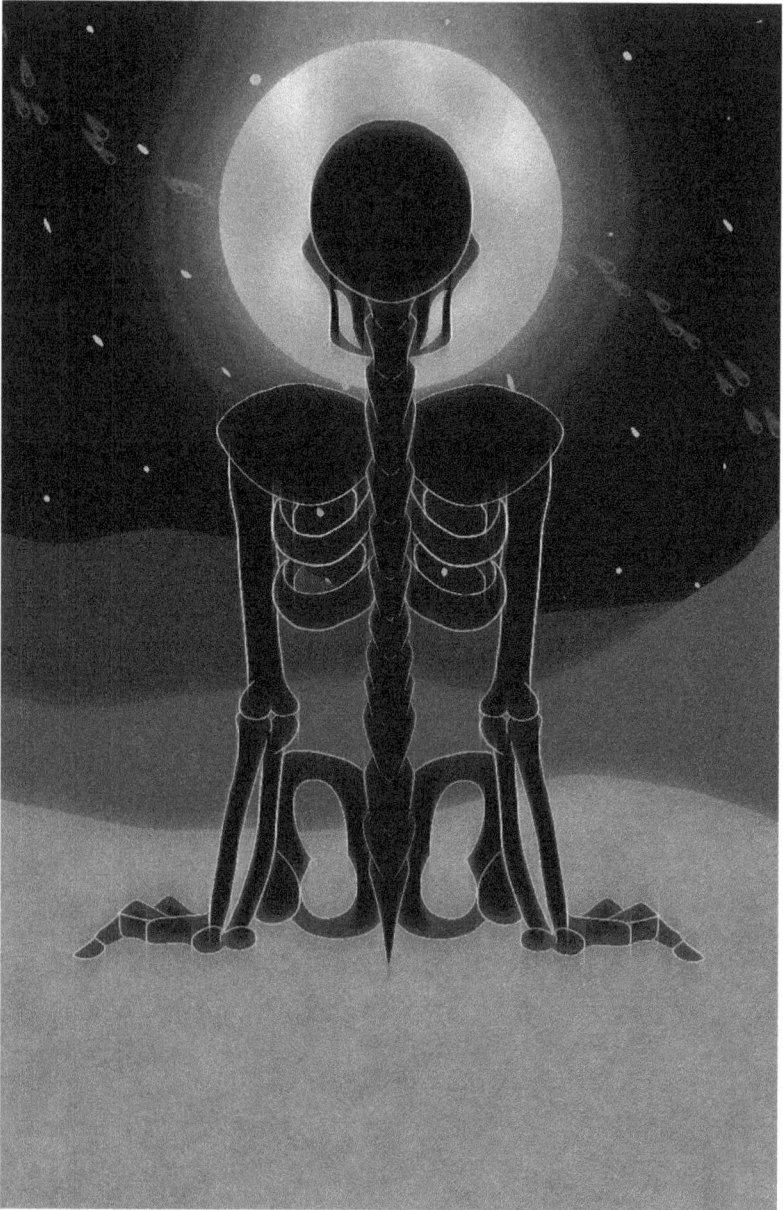

The Wasteland

A starting point that occurs early and sometimes late in life. It is a place we know we must leave. Though perhaps we'd like to stay, content in its familiarity and comfort, on a visceral level, we know we must go.

A Long Way From Home

Ain't no water in my well no more,
ain't no honey in the comb
and I am just a poor boy
a long way from home.
Ain't no sugar in the gourd for me,
and it don't matter where I'm from
cause I am just a poor boy
a long way from home.

Was I blind in this life,
will I see once I am gone.
Will I walk a hard road,
and sing a broken song
or will my voice lie silent,
and quiet as a stone
because I'm just a poor boy,
a long way from home.

Jezebel can you hold me,
through my trouble and my woe
or do you love me falsely,
though I will never know.
You loved me with your flesh,
but did you love me in your bones
or was I just a poor boy,
a long way from home.

I was way down in the narrows,
in the valley of the gun,
the serpent's tongue upon my face,
like the heat of the desert Sun.
Yahweh-Elah-Elohim,
don't leave me here alone
don't forsake this poor boy,
a long way from home.

A Madman in the Desert

I saw a Madman in the desert
but I didn't see no swine
and all that he would say to me was
"Have you seen my Clementine."
and yonder down the canyon
was a rider on a Pale Horse
and he said "All of those who wander,
aren't necessarily lost."

So, I walked on into the valley
down in the shadows don't you see
and though I heard the voices
I don't think they were speaking to me.
From the Pedro you can see DogTown
across the Border Fence
And again, I heard the voices,
but they didn't make no sense.

They said they saw Ol' Massaw,
up and walkin' like a man
Had an opium pipe in his pocket
and a six gun in his hand.
He said "two trains used to run here,
way back in the day.
One ran down to Mexico
and the other just ran away."

I got Jesus on a necklace,
got his Mama on there too
and sometimes I'm not sure about
whose feet are in my shoes.
and I walked up and down the Pedro
'til the Moon began to shine.
Just a Madman in the desert,
Lookin' for Clementine.

Ain't Nothin' 'Round Here (But Trouble)

They ain't nothing round here but trouble
cause trouble always comes one day
and all them lowdown sinners
hopin' trouble don't come their way.

And my Brother, he dreams of the bottle
and I only dream of the gun.
We are both eternal children
though no longer are we young.

I saw crows out over the desert
and whales in the deep blue sea.
I heard a voice in the belly of Leviathan
that said "Lord, have mercy on me."

I walked the road that leads to Perdition,
I been on the road to Jubilee,
I heard songs in the Houses of the Holy
sung by people I could not see.

And I went down in the dark ol' midnight
Just to see what I could see.
They ain't nothin' round here but trouble
Nothin' but trouble and me.

Blues for Moses

And I looked over yonder
and saw the judgement at hand
Go down Moses
into Canaan's land
I saw crows black all over
round the grave digger man
Go down Moses
into Canaan's land

I heard a voice say Peter
won't you cut them nails
Go down Moses
with the Holy Grail
Pick up that single cone
and make it wail
Go down Moses
with the Holy Grail

With a white oak on the left
and the crossroads on the right
Go down Moses
with the Israelites
With ol' Legba in the middle
down in the dark ol' midnite
Go down Moses
with the Israelites

Ain't goin' down that big road
all by myself
Moses shouts in anger
at the golden calf
Gonna put my sinful ways
back up on the shelf
Moses shouts in anger
at the golden calf

John the revelator and the levee camp moan
Moses in the wilderness all alone
My black mama said be home by sundown
Moses in the wilderness all alone

Dead Men, Guns, and Morphine

Out in the canyons of that Sonoran Land,
the desert can clear you to the very last man.
Still, it ain't the worst place that I ever been.
Down with the dead men,
the guns, and the morphine.

Massaw wants to walk the skin off my bones
and leave me in the wasteland all alone,
But he still ain't the worst thing that I ever seen.
Down with the dead men,
the guns, and the morphine.

And the trouble comes hard in a hard ol' land
like a hammer on the nails at the Crucifix-ee-an.
Tellin' the truth ain't as easy as it seems.
To the dead men,
the guns, and the morphine.

I heard YaWeh on the mountain,
heard His hammer ring
Saw the Baptist on the Pedro,
heard the choir start to sing
Said He'd shatter my chains into smithereens
Down with the dead men,
the guns and the morphine.

I was watchin' the Moon
as it cut through the night
Like a knife on the Altars
of the Israelites
7 and 7 and 7 it seems.
Beats the dead men,
the guns, and the morphine.

Down on the Pedro

Where you been so long,
I been looking high and low
Seems like I'll never find you
wanderin' down on the Pedro
I've walked my face into the wind
and my eye into the Moon
I've walked this river so long
I better see you pretty soon
Down on the Pedro

Won't you roll them bones
cause the crows don't care
Out there flyin'
around in the air
And the swine don't worry
about your pearls don't you know
It's a whole 'nother world
down here on the Pedro
Down on the Pedro

When you're watchin' your shadow
in the pale moonlight
Doin' what you gotta
before the day gets too bright
Turn your wine into water
and golden idols back into clay
Get your work all done
before the break of day
Down on the Pedro

The Earth is patient
and the river is slow
From all that misery
comin' up out of Mexico
Don't worry 'bout your footprints
stayin' in the sand all day
cause the monsoon comes along
and washes them all away
Down on the Pedro

Lonely Graves

What are we 'sposed to do now,
we got nowhere to run
Gonna end up lookin' at Heaven
over the barrel of a gun
I was lonely when you got here
and I'll be lonely when you go
I'm gonna get up out this hole
and walk to Jericho

I would do anything you told me,
I'd believe anything you say
If I could just get up again
out of this lonely grave
I would try to feed the hungry
and shelter those alone
I would comfort those in sorrow
and lead the lost ones home

I wanna roll my aging bones
right down that whiskey road
Take seat up at the bar
and watch the drama that unfolds

Walkin' out the graveyard
in my dirty dyin' shoes
Everything looks good
when you got nothing left to lose

And if I get too far out there
down South and all alone
I can float back on the Pedro
when I feel like comin' home
I may be just a dead man
out walkin' in the Sun
But in the Valley of Elah
I won't be the only one

I've committed every single sin
that you might care to call
And I don't have the fingers to even
try to count them all
But down in the old religion
all my transgressions are gone
Fallin' down away from me
like barley from a millin' stone

Out in Babylon

First time I saw her
she looked like trouble
First time I saw her
she looked like pain
Like a broken ankle
stuck down in the rubble
When I first saw Babylon

Way down in the river
where the dark fish lay
Way up where the Moon don't shine
Way down in the ground
where the snakes crawl away
Way out in Babylon

Dust in your lungs
and dust in your soul
The scales fall away one by one
It's never the same
as what you been told
Once you been to Babylon

I've seen Saints turned into sinners
Look around at what we've done
We're all losers cause there ain't no winners
Out here in Babylon

I'm gonna pray in the sand
by the river so wide
Pray till the Sun goes down
If I can just make it to the other side
I can get out of Babylon

Prayin' for Rain

Listen to the whisper of the gun in my hand
Listen to the morphine in my veins
Listen to the voices in the Promised Land
Listen to me Prayin' for Rain

Old Moses down in Egypt's Land
Out on the burnin' plain
The first thing He told Israel
Was to get down and Pray for Rain

Can't Baptize nobody in a dried-up wash
A dry field don't grow no grain
Gotta wait for high water raisin' on up
When everybody Prays for Rain

Go down old Noah with your two by twos
Down with your crosscut and your plane
Ain't gonna' float that Gopher Wood
If you don't see no Rain

Down in the rushin' waters
Where we all end up again
Down in the Old Religion
Down here Prayin' for Rain

UnderLand

All my sorrows
Are gone like a dead man's tomorrows
And I flowed like water
through an iniquitous hand
Down to the UnderLand

And the Arc Angel told me
Don't believe the stories that are sold to me
Told me to look for the grave digger man
When I find myself in the UnderLand

Told the Lord I done slipped my chain
Runnin' like a rabbit in the rain
But I broke the grip of the devil's hand
When I was down in the UnderLand

And I saw the mornin' light
Gonna lead me out of the dark ol' midnite
Leadin' me to the Baptist's hand
Down in the UnderLand

I looked out over the river so deep
To the top of YahWeh's mountain so steep
Felt that jawbone in my killin' hand
When I was down in the UnderLand

Road of Crosses

I can see a Grave yard
all the tombstones in my eyes
The Angels all are cryin'
with the crosses rollin' by
The Boulevard is a one-way street
and if you walk you'll wish you'd ran
You'll get to know the feel
of a grave spade in your hand

Down in the dirt
and down in the ground
Old Man Holy,
he can't always be around
Down in the murder hole,
down with the black cat bones
Out on the road of crosses
where the fallen sleep alone

Way out in the wilderness
in the Hinterland of old
In the belly of the whale
and from the lion's den I'm told
You can see the road of crosses
stretching into the night
All the plastic flowers
and the candles burning bright

Down in the dirty water,
baptized in the rain
Down in the old religion
where we all end up again
Out on the road of crosses
where the lighted candles stand
You can hear the footsteps
headed to the Promised Land

Santa Pistolera

And far off in the distance
I could hear a Conjunto band
Singing a Corrida
about a Woman's vengeful hand

In honor of her sisters
who were murdered upon the way
Back home to friends and family
at the end of a working day

Santa Pistolera
No law can stay your hand
As you send one more el violador
Down into the sand

They were our Mothers and our Daughters
and our Sisters and our Wives
Who worked so hard to feed us
then paid for it with their lives

They fell like leaves in Autumn
along the dusty road
While the engines of perdition
traveled to and fro

But for every Woman crying,
there is a Huntress comes
To slay one more el violador
for the evil that was done

The Journey

Illustrates our steps out of the Wasteland. Tentative, lonely, and unsure, we are irrevocably compelled to place one foot in front of the other. And as we travel, we realize what stands in our way, becomes the way.

And Faith Will Take You

And the Moon looks like a sickle
at the Reaper's Jamboree
It's gonna light my way
on the road to Jubilee
Don't you worry about the words
that got wrote down in that book
Faith will give you what you need
when you're takin your last look

And Faith is gonna take you
where you need to be
Gonna put your walkin' shoes
up on the road to Galilee
And Faith is gonna take you
all the way to the end
And leave you on the doorstep
to that ol' Promised Land

One hand on the hammer
and one hand on the nails
One man with the lions
and one man in the whale

Fourth man in a fire
that can never be burned
And one man with a millstone
that ain't never gonna turn

There is a beast in this ol' house
that's just itchin' to break free
and the only chains that hold it
are the ones that are held by me
There's rain in this house
way up underneath the roof
and a TV in the hallway
that don't ever tell the truth

And I want to forge a killin' sword
just like ol' Tubal Cain
but I'm stuck here in this furnace
that I made with my own hands
I need high water forgiveness
for my low water sins
and only Faith will get me out
of this furnace that I'm in

And Legion is My Name

Gabriel oh Gabriel
with your foot on the land and sea
I am headed to Perdition
and praying for Jubilee
I have King James in my pocket
and Smith and Wesson in my hand
And I am just a sinner
headed to the Promised Land

I wear a coat of many colors
and a yoke of many troubles
I have a voice like many waters
and Legion is my name
I have the drivin' thirst of a drowning man
a jawbone in my killing hand
To slay the wicked out on the sand
and Legion is my name

I got one hand in the fire
and gonna shake and shout
I got the other down in Canaan
Tryin' to pull you out

I got hot foot powder spillin'
outa both my shoes
and a 32-20 that'll kill you
through and through

I'm moppin' up the killin' floor
from the work I done
Fillin' in the Murder Hole
and then I'm up and gone
Jesus on the Main Line
said his hand is there for me
Reach up from my dyin' bed
and He's gonna pull me free

I'm a man among the many,
a leaf among the trees
I am sand upon the desert
and dust upon the breeze
Selah, Selah, Selah,
when I'm layin' in that clay
He said He's comin' back around
to pick me up one day

Find My Way Home

They said they had the answers
on this television show
About a man and his money,
and how he needed some more
and the tears rolled like rain
down weathered ol' faces
And hearts rose like hawks
from the falconer's jesses

You can look through a shot glass
and see your soul
While you listen to the Devil
on the radio
and the dust of the ages
gonna move you along
While you wear out your shoes
tryin' to find your way home

But the Word came down
in the dark ol' midnite
Ain't nobody leaves
when they turn out the lights

And the Spirit's gonna move me,
don't know where I'm goin'
But I'm wearin' out my shoes
Tryin' to find my way home

The view you get
from the Crucifixion Tree
Ain't worth the money
or the misery
But it'll be all worth it
when they take you down
With a hole in your side
and your life blood gone

I wanna send my Soul
down the river to the Sea
and roll with the ages
till they set me free
In the Baptismal Water
with my Soul full of rain
Like weathered ol' Faces
when the Hawks fly again

Jericho Bound

And that train kept a rollin'
down the LRT line
Don't stop by the lonely graves
cause you're only wastin' time
And I knew my train was comin'
when I heard that whistle blow
As it rolled into the station
headed down to Jericho

I was ragged in the wilderness
like a bleached and dyin' tree
But you can't judge my heart
until you've walked a mile with me
Straight into the crossfire
with a gun in both your hands
Shootin' all that's evil
on your way to the Promised Land

And where were you just standin'
when the World was burnin' down
Did you buy a one-way ticket
but then just threw it on the ground

Will you look down at your battered feet
to see just where they are
Torn like ragged harpies
in a dirty, rundown bar

I read the Book of Ezekiel
like the lines in my own hand
Like a hafted sword that flashed
 and shone all throughout the land
Don't worry about the leaven
that I got in my bread
Or the Host that rests inside my mouth
or the oil on my head

Can you hear the trumpets
way out in Jericho
Or is it that old whistle
I keep hearin' don't you know
Rollin on down to Judgement
sure as night'll turn to day
Don't wait out by the lonely graves,
or you'll only lose your way

Mexican BlackBird Down to the Sea

The rain fell like judgement
on a faithless Jezebel
And the wind hurled insults
so that you couldn't really tell
Where the exit off the highway was,
South on 83
The turn for the Mexican BlackBird
all the way down to the Sea

I was runnin' when I got here
I'll be runnin' when I go
You didn't see me when I got here,
and you won't see me anymore
I'm leavin' early in the morning
'bout the break of day, you'll see
Headin' down the BlackBird
all the way down to the Sea.

Jack Straw from Wichita
rode a freight to a shallow grave
South bound to a hole in the ground
and he couldn't really be saved

Just a step or two outside the law
Thinkin' he was free
He's buried on the BlackBird
on the way down to the Sea

Take me to the Pedro
Runnin' north out of Mexico
Baptize me in the Righteous Blood
and the Holy Milagros
Bless me at the crossroads
beneath a white oak tree
And deliver me down the BlackBird
all the way down to the Sea

I will fear no evil,
and I will fear no man
I have the Sword of Ezekiel
hafted to my hand
I no longer fear the reaper
 now that my soul has been set free
To wander down the BlackBird
all the way down to the Sea

Out in the Hard Country

And I would ride the high iron
on the rails down to the Sea
A solitary hobo
out in the hard country
It's a long way past the river
down where I need to be
When you're a solitary hobo
out in the hard country

The Angel asked if I was Water,
I said I'm the vessel to be filled
He said are you the Wheel,
I said I'm barley to be milled
He asked if I was Fire,
and I said I'm the burning Land
He called me a Killer,
but I'm just the Killer's hand

I heard that lonesome whistle
outside the Church House late last night
Sleeping by the Altar
waitin' on the morning light

That train kept a rollin'
out in the darkness before dawn
And a solitary hobo
is getting up and getting gone

Everybody's always talkin'
about the things they've never seen
Wishin' they could travel
to a place they never been
I wanna roll in those waters
of the flood where Noah stood
But I always end up going
where I said I never would

In my pocket there's a dollar,
the last one that I own
But there ain't no place to spend it
down in the valley of the bones
But all my lamps are trimmed
and burnin' down in the valley of the Gun
There ain't no need to worry
when you got no place to run

Revelation Train

I fell asleep one evening
down by the Fairbank Station Line
And I dreamed the Revelation Train
was rollin' through my mind

And I saw the Hobo Nation
standin' all along the track
And that train up and took them
all away and never brought them back

The Revelation Train was rollin'
down through that Border Land
And the steam what came out the Engine
was in the shape of Yahweh's Hand

I heard the sound of boxcars
Rollin' like guns in the killin' ground
And I knew that Ol' Man Holy
was fixin' to come around

And I dreamed I saw a Crow fly,
blacker than the night
Straight up outta Mexico
ahead of the mornin' light

Ahead of the Revelation Train
but it ain't goin' my way
Even though we all got tickets
I won't be using mine today

Ain't but the one train runnin'
that'll take you all away
Leavin' once at midnite
and once at the break of day

The one time that I saw it
painted all over white
Headed for the bone yard
down in the dark ol' midnight

Sinner's Train

I heard that .44 whistle blowin'
Out in that Sonoran land
And I felt that ol' morphine flowin'
To the pistol in my hand

I got them Sodom and Gomorrah Blues
Way down in my Soul
Wastin' time that I could' a used
Lookin' for that ol' jellyroll

The Sinner's Train rolled like thunder
Out across that no man's land
And I heard them blues in the way down under
Up and walkin' like a man

Listen to my Single Cone
And my Coricidin Slide
Wake up all them restless bones
Down in the dark ol' midnite

I saw two trains a runnin'
But one already gone
Took away the only Woman
That I could ever call my own

Gonna Ride on Through

Heard my Greyhound Bus a comin'
Straight up that Highway 92
Gonna take me out to Fairbank
But I believe I'll just ride on through

I met a woman with snakes in her hair
Standin' in the Evenin' Sun
Told me I was gonna get old one day
If I didn't end up dyin' young

I got whiskey socks and morphine shoes
Gonna carry me to the Promised Land
I got a suit coat made of gabardine
And a Smith and Wesson in my hand

I got a Death Letter in my pocket
And the Book of Enoch too
I'll ride that Greyhound through the crossroads
If ol' Legba will let me through

But if St. Peter doesn't let me pass
I don't know what I'm gonna do
Guess I'll stay on that ol' Greyhound
And try to ride on through

This Old Railroad

This old Railroad has got me down
And this old hammer weighs 100 pounds
I want to leave this life
and move back into Town
'Cause this old Railroad has got me down

Ocean Boy stayed out with the old machines
He said "Call me The Bird,
'cause I got these wings"
And he flew so fast
that I heard the Rail Lines sing
And he carried an old tin can
full of dangerous things

I never moved an inch from where I stand
And the Wolf never sleeps
in this hungry old land
The Pass Over Angel
never tips his hand
Till you drop down Mama
dead in the Desert Sand

I want that Baptismal Water
to wash me clean again
When I finally walk out of the Lion's Den
I want to sing "Wayfarin' Stranger", and then
I want to walk them cross ties
down until they end

Jack Straw from Wichita said to me
I believe that you and I can now agree
Ain't no railroad train gonna set you free
If you ain't where you think you want to be

Who is Funeral Jane?

There are far too many candles
in the Cathedral of my pain
Though Holy Water washes
every pew and floorboard clean

I asked of every Angel
before they began to sing
But none of them could tell me,
"Who is Funeral Jane?"

I put money in the collection plate
and lit a votive in the rain
I said a small oration
with a Milagro in my hand

And I heard that lonesome whistle
on a West bound hobo train
But still, no one could tell me,
"Who is Funeral Jane?"

I saw some rubber trampers
out on the windy plains
As they hoboed on to Iowa
and hoboed back again

I asked the reigning King and Queen
as they drank from old tin cans
But neither one could tell me,
"Who is Funeral Jane?"

There's a portrait drawn in charcoal
on every single train
That asks of every drifter,
"Do you know this man?"

A riddle in a boxcar
where a rail dog was slain
Beside him in the dust appeared
"Who is Funeral Jane?"

The Enlightenment

Occurs, to one degree or another, as we encounter and resolve impediments to our Journey. Calm and simplicity elude us as we overthink, overreact, and overstep, only to realize in the end that our original efforts were the correct ones.

cj fletcher

As the Crow Flies

And I saw one evening way up in the sky
The Crows that were flyin' before my eyes

Down through the valley of the gun they flew
Along the San Pedro then they disappeared
    from view

Black all over out from under the night
Out of the Desert and into the Sunlight

I baked me some bread like Ezekiel by the
    shore
I ate it all up and then I baked me some more

I been laid on my side for all these days
Waitin' on YahWeh to take my troubles away

And all along the Pedro I watched the people
   come
Like sinners walkin' out of Jerusalem

I want to walk into Canaan
with the Israelites
But I'm stuck with the Crows
over the Desert in Flight

And I heard the Prophet tell me
as the sun began to set
You can walk on down to Glory
But you ain't got there yet

Gonna See Your Good Man Gone

I never cared about money,
it's just a stone in my shoes
A dollar don't buy you nothin'
down in the Valley of the Blues
I been out in the Nations
where they got more skin than bones
And I heard they're all just waitin'
to see a good man gone

I remember I told you never to go
Down where the Peavine whistle blows
Down by the Murder Hole
fulla' Black Cat Bones
Down where they're hopin'
to see a good man gone

And I saw those feral children running,
lest they be devoured
They didn't have a word for evil,
so they just borrowed ours
And when the light bled down
from that settin' Sun
I watched those children run headlong
after a good man gone

I saw a Gray Cat sleepin'
under a mesquite tree
Way down yonder in the valley
where the dogs ran free
There are two trains runnin'
out of the Valley of Bones
Past a lonely woman cryin'
"Where's my good man gone"

I heard the Prophet tell me,
the time is comin' soon
Gonna see me some salt pillars
under the desert Moon
And down by that San Pedro
I seen them fugitives run
Straight on past the Prophet
to see a good man gone

If You Hear Me Singin'

And if you hear me singin'
All them old church house songs
I'm only tryin' to show you
What it takes to get along

The rain fell hard in that desert land
Like a wooden ruler across an orphan's hand
And I looked through the rain
and out past my tears
And thought that I'd do anything
to finally get out of here

I heard a shot out in the canyon
like a rollin' thunderhead
They said it was The Devil
and I knew someone was dead
And the World don't ever change
as far as I can see
They either got my money
or they got a hold of me

And I heard The Prophet tell me
"What are you worried about"?
Many have gone before you
and they all did without
There was a black all over crow said
"The Sun don't shine at night
And the Moon is just a mirror
for someone else's light"

And I was walkin' out of Mexico
while the Moon shone bright
Straight on up the Pedro
under someone else's light
And I heard that Blues Man singing
all them old Chain Gang songs
But he was only tryin'
to show me what it takes to get along

Inside My Skin

The Devil is always waitin'
You know he never sleeps
You can see the empty cartridges
Scattered round his cloven feet

You can hear the Desert speaking
With a voice like a growlin' dog
I heard his ancient poetry
Though I didn't catch it all

And way down in the narrows
Down where you ain't got no friends
I got everything I'll ever need
Right here inside my skin

And I saw that Passover Angel
Down in that Sonoran land
Flyin' over the Desert
With a six gun in his hand

And He told me you could see it
That Ol' Promised Land out there
But I couldn't see a thing you see
With all the gun smoke in the air

Justified Tonight
(Collaboration with Mandie Gaynor)

Long shadows fall before me
Walkin' in these sinner's shoes
Can't see the light behind you
While you're payin' all your dues

Too many dark Moons and not enough shine
To light my feet on their way
Another dollar down but the pots finally right
I got no debts left to pay

Two nickels here ain't worth a dime
Two wrongs don't make a right
But I learned how to kill two birds at one time
So I'm feelin' justified tonight

The river bends but it never breaks
While it rushes Southward bound
But even roaring waters will slow and disappear
And seep into the ground

Looking in the Western sky
Out at the Burning Sun
All my sorrows are falling away
Now that my trials are done

Mexodus

I heard those old Corridos comin'
in way down low
Through the static and hiss
of that desert radio
And when those tubes get hot
all the way up inside
That old radio smells
just like formaldehyde

And didn't My Lord deliver Daniel
from the lions long ago
In them old Bible stories
that you don't hear no more
Did he not deliver David
from a giant on the sand
Why not every people,
why not every man

There's a Blood Moon crossin'
over the border tonight
Lookin' down on the pilgrims
over the desert in flight
And Old Man Holy is lookin' down the line
To see if that Fairbank Train is on time

I seen Old Moses
with his eyes full of sand
While Santa Muerta
brings the pilgrims out of Pharaoh's Land
And Jesus Malverde
stands in the mornin' light
Waitin' on the sunshine
walkin' out of the midnite

And all the roads that will lead you
to the promised land
Are leveled by the spade
of the Grave Digger Man
And I heard that old Corrido
Comin' in low
Through the static and the hiss
of my desert radio

Minute Man

Did you ever see the graves
on a Full Moon night
They look like teeth
in the Devil's underbite
And I wish I could fly
the way a black crow might
Across the face of the Moon
in flight

I'm gonna wash these hands
that will never be clean
Maybe just enough
to save my skin
I know where I come from
and know where I've been
There ain't enough numbers
to count my sins

Go Down Old Moses,
would you ever stand
Out in the desert
with a gun in your hand

Or would you watch those people
to the very last man
Run head long into
the promised land

I never did all the things I should
Not even half of what I said I would
But after tonight, they'll know where I stood
They'll know that I did the best that I could

Goin' out in the Desert
where you don't want to go
Gonna learn some things
you don't wanna know
And if I wondered why
no one knew my name before
I'll have a new one when
I cross to that other shore

Ocean Boy

And I looked out over the water
and looked on out to sea
All I saw was Ocean Boy
looking back at me

I said Hey, Hey, what do the big fish say
Down in the Pago Pago gales
There ain't no Joy for Ocean Boy
'Til they spit him outta the Whale

Ocean Boy moved on the Seven Seas
like a ship from a faraway land
He said "There's no sorrow or trouble for me"
as he stepped out on to the sand

I said Hey, Hey, down Mexico
way Down in the Gaderenes
Ain't no Joy for Ocean Boy
If he ain't on the Seven Seas

And the Sun shone down on the sea foam
like diamonds in the morning light
The sea lions swam with Ocean Boy
out of the dark ol' midnite

He said Hey, Hey, down Aruba way
Down in the Yucatans
There ain't no Joy, said Ocean Boy
Down in them Desert Lands

Way off in the distance
I heard an ol' sea lion roar
And I knew that it was Ocean Boy
swimmin' in to shore

Old Machines

When all of the engines
finally run out of steam
And all of the cars
run out of gasoline
It don't really matter
that you don't know what it means
When you're down
with the old machines

A bucket full of oil
and a bucket full of rust
A bucket full of ashes
and a bucket full of dust
And my tires are worn smooth
from the weight of my sins
Tryin' to roll that
righteous mileage in

One drink of whiskey
and two drinks of gin
Was an old machine
put me in the place I'm in

Chasin' the Dragon
and turned to the morphine
Took me all the way down
with the old machines

I found an old tin can
full of dangerous things
Down in the valley
of the old machines
I knew that Ocean Boy
had been out that way
Down in the valley
for a year and a day

I heard it on the radio
down in the dark ol' midnite
The carousel stopped
and turned out its lights
That old machine took me
all the way round the World
And turned out my pockets
like an old whiskey girl

Over in Rabbit Land

Later Gators,
on down the road, my friend
You don't need no ticket
to ride this train
Goin' down to the station
with my suitcase in my hand
Gonna catch that southbound all the way
over to Rabbit Land

She can cook up porkchops
and bake gingerbread
Or toast them marshmallows
If you want that instead
The menu is on the Frigidaire
wrote down in her own hand
You don't wanna be late for supper
Down in Rabbit Land

She's got a Minecraft City
painted all over green
And She sleeps all night
on a trampoline

She's got a cat named Houston
painted all over tan
Helps himself to tacos
over in Rabbit Land

She's got a see through heart
made out of chewin' gum
And 25 dogs
in her Minecraft room
She lets Stampy Cat do the talkin'
with her tablet in her hand
And She draws lots of pictures
over in Rabbit Land

They call her the Rabbit
and the Blue Kangaroo
She's got a cat on her backpack
when She heads off to school
You can see her on the playground
with a magic 8-ball in her hand
Answerin' all the questions
down in Rabbit Land

Spirit and Flesh

And there are songs of the Spirit
and there are songs of the Flesh
And there are songs that you sing
when you got nothin' left

You can sing them up high
and sing them way down low
Some you can sing when you got
nowhere else to go

Down in the old Religion
where the Heathens all stand
They'd rather have a killer
than an upright preacher man

Down where sins weigh heavy
every day of your life
Dull and achin' like the edge
of an old butcher knife

I've been out on the sea
on a ship with midnite sails
I been in the valley of the shadow
with a posse on my trail

I flew like a crow
through the mountains and the hills
And I took to the Morphine
with the lowdown shakin' chills

I laid down with Belladonna
and had the Wolf Bane dreams
I was 40 days in the desert
where the Jimson Weed screams

I saw Samson with his jawbone
and the Reaper with his scythe
Playin' Mexican Train and "42"
down in the dark ol' Midnite

The Killer's Hymn

Six dark horses
will draw me away
With six bright bullets
on the Judgement Day
I used to think that I
would live by the gun
But it seems I am a killer
with my guitar and my songs

A well full of water
and I can't drink
A schoolhouse full of books
and I still can't think
A kitchen full of food
and I can't eat
Ain't enough road
underneath my feet

Sorrow in the wasteland
where no one can hear
Gonna pick up my troubles
and walk away from there

I'm never gonna follow you
no matter what it takes
I ain't gonna wake up
in a bed I didn't make

Trouble gonna come
sure as the trumpets sound
Gonna bury my sins
in a hole in the ground
Gonna bury you too
if you get in my way
Sure as the night
gonna turn into day

Ain't nothing more dangerous
than the unseen hand
That belongs to the body
of a guitar man
Six bright strings
gonna carry you away
And walk you to the wasteland
on Judgement Day.

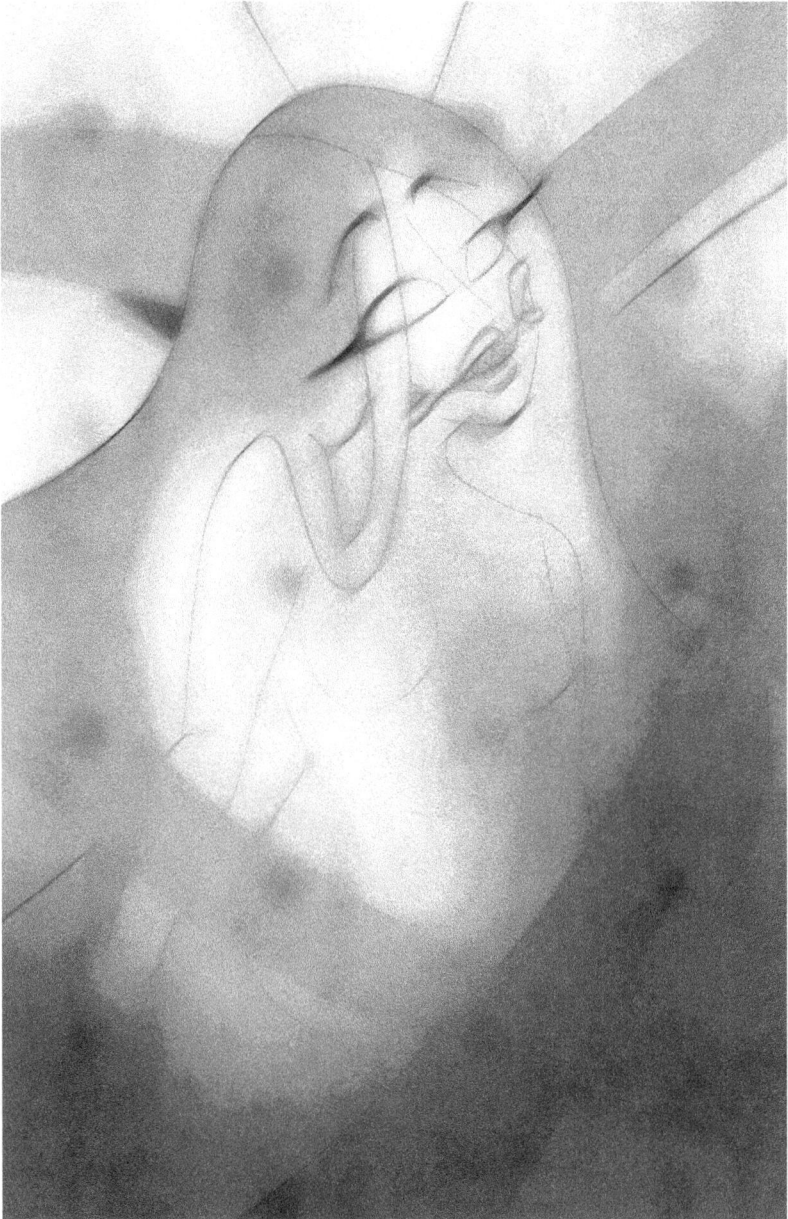

The Salvation

Comes when, with no one else to turn to, nowhere else to go, and nothing else to do, in our Enlightened state, we realize we have traveled to the place where we began ... The Wasteland.

Balada Oscura

Never mind the darkness
when the Moon comes out to play
Gonna show you all the shadows
you don't see in the light of day

Stuck in the rhythms
of your old ancient ways
Lonely and cruel
down where The Prophet stays

Balada Oscura,
I got nothin' left to say
I got more past than future,
ain't that just the way

Balada Oscura
I heard The Prophet say
You got more past than future,
ain't that always the way

And I saw them Narco Saints
down by the old San Pedro
Scattered through the Desert
like they didn't know where to go

Them Black Sheep walk at midnite
out of the land of sorrow
Ahead of the hungry,
headed for tomorrow

But I can fly like a bird
when I kneel down to pray
Maybe Ol' Man Holy
gonna listen to what I say

And I saw the Revelation Train
leave the station today
They rounded up the sinners
and took them all away

Desert Apostle

Way down yonder
in the Border Land
The Apostle wrote scripture
in the Desert sand
He said down by the river
that rolls from the sea
Down by the river
they're gonna bury me

The road don't run
beneath my feet no more
Down in the valley
my time is o'er
Two crows flyin'
mean no sorrow for me
Seven crows flyin'
gonna set me free

Down by the river
that rolls from the sea
Down in the river
where they baptized me

And my house in the valley
is empty and cold
Down in the valley
where I grew so old

Valley of Miracles, Valley of the gun
The Apostle wrote scripture
under the Desert Sun
When the last of the Believers
leave this barren land
The Word of the Apostle
still burns in the sand

Ol' Saint Peter
don't you still your hand
When you see the Apostle
from the Burning Land
Oh, Saint Peter
don't you stay your hand
Write down his name
in the burning sand

In the Trouble No More

The rain fell hard
down on the desert sand
Like Justice through the fingers
of a killer's hand

And I heard
that Jericho Trumpet sound
Heard the Rumble and the roar
when the walls came down

I heard those old voices
from so long ago
Comin up out the ground
from way down below

Like listenin' to The Prophet
on an old radio
Down in the trouble
no more

I been down in the narrows
lookin' for a home
Jesus made up my dyin' bed
while I was up and gone

And I high stepped to the Mansion,
to the House of Many Rooms
And Cakewalked my way out
of the Valley of Tombs

I heard The Prophet tell me
I had nothin' left to lose
Walkin' like a hobo
down in the Land of the Blues

I said I want to run
like a Rabbit through the rain
Like water through the fingers
of the Baptizer Man

Ghost Town

I'm gonna get this dust from offa my bones
And the rust from outta my blood
Break the chains that held me to these sinner's
    stones
In the ghost town where I stood

I thought I heard a Woman cryin'
But that was just the wind
Since I have been delivered
From the ghost town I was in

Don't cut my name in no markin' stone
But keep the candles burnin' bright
When I walk out from the valley of bones
And leave the ghosts behind tonight

Never been no others to take my place
Underneath that martyr's crown
I got back up when I fell from grace
And walked away from the killin' ground

A burnin' bush and bread and wine
A table amidst my enemies
I've left my burdens so far behind
In the ghost town that was me

God Walks on the Sand

And God moved across the waters
And he walked across the land
And he delivered every enemy
Into the palm of my open hand

I will walk down to the battle
A sword unto my hand
And souls will be shaken
When God walks upon the sand

I want to walk out to Babel
Just to step on the land
And holler YahWeh, Elah, Elohim
As He walks upon the sand

A tear upon white linen
Blood upon a shroud
I shall depart back whence I came
Like a cloud

As I stand out in the wilderness
There ain't no place of ease
But I will do my forty years
As pretty as you please

Gonna Be Alright

Hard times are comin'
but they always come and go
Hard times wanna come
at me the way a river flows
And the Nations always ride
on the back of a workin' man
And salvation always seems
to come with a pistol in it's hand

All your sins
for all your tomorrows
Get wrote down hard
in the Book of Sorrows
I'm gonna wait 'til All Hallows
to talk to them souls
I learned how by readin'
the Dead Sea Scrolls

I read the Book of Enoch,
read how the Angels fell
Down to hard luck and trouble
where beautiful women dwell

And I would forge that iron
like ol' Tubal Cain
And I would fell the wicked
like candles in the rain

The road out of Eden
is a hard and broken track
You can still see all the footprints
but ain't none goin' back
And way out West of Heaven
in that hard rock mountainside
Were Angels with savage weapons
watching over those who died

And far off in the distance
I saw a Great Speckled Bird
I asked a simple question
but she wouldn't say a word
But there were two Crows flyin'
out from under the night
They said there ain't no need to worry,
It's all gonna be alright

Gypsy Girl

I was a shadow in the Desert
at the House of Autumn Leaves
Bangin' on the door
until it opened for me
I have a heart full of Winter
caught in the Summer rain
Trapped like an old-time sinner
down in the Old Religion

Thought I saw my Gypsy Girl
by the Sea of Galilee
But that might be just a dream
that faded like dust upon the breeze
I know you made them crazy
all the way down in their bones
You left 'em all just wanderin'
in the wasteland all alone

Down in the lowlands
I saw that Gypsy Girl
Heard her name's been spoken
all over the World

Maria Magdalena
down in the Valley of Crimes
Walkin' with the Pilgrims
'til they all ran out of time

Thought I saw you holdin'
an alabaster jar
Thought I heard those old Oracians
way down in the dark
And I was crazy in the graveyard
down in the Gadarenes
Couldn't see that Gypsy Girl
while the swine all stood about me

You drew the flock to The Shepherd,
You drew tears to my eyes
You drew blood to the Chalice
with thunder in the skies
I thought I saw you sittin'
high in that upper room
I thought I saw you standin'
by that hollow empty tomb

House Made of Stone

I wanna live in a house made of stone
But I wake up in a house afire
Walkin' to the house of many mansions alone
I end up at the house of desire

Down in your dreams
where the flames rise higher
and the Angel cracks
the seal on the scroll
The wolf is walkin' round
inside your chicken wire
While you listen
to the Church Bell toll

Sometimes that ol' Smith and Wesson
Is the only friend you know
And the narrow road to Heaven
Is the only place left to go

Down in the barrens where anything goes
The chaff stays tight to the wheat
And you never hear the horn of plenty blow
Till it knocks you off your feet

And I would ride that Revelation train
Down through the Desert Sand
And I will slip like monsoon rain
Through the fingers of a sinner's hand

Old Religion

I never heard the voice of Adam,
never heard the voice of the snake
But if I die before I do,
I pray the Lord my soul to take

Down in the Old Religion
Down where two worlds meet
It'll tear the yoke from off your neck
and take shackles off your feet

and I was just a vessel
out on the Sea of Galilee
and The Lord said "Float like Gopher Wood
straight on back to Me"

Thought I saw a Crow flyin'
blacker than the night
He flew into the sunrise
and vanished in the light

I saw the world of the Red Man
up and raptured away
Saw it turn to murder
and gin and apathy

I saw the Tower of Babel
out on the desert sand
And I saw the Warrior Angels
with six-guns in their hands

And then I heard the Gabriel Trumpet,
over the sound of all the guns
I saw all the Saints and Sinners,
and they all spoke in tongues

Pale Horse

Ol' YahWeh said to Moses
throw that stick down on the ground
I saw it turn into a snake
and start to crawl around

I saw a pale horse walkin'
out on the Meggido sand
Walked amongst the fallen,
down to the very last man

I saw blood up to my knees
out on the Meggido Line
Gonna wash it all away,
but none of it was mine

And far off in the distance
thought I heard that Shofar blow
They said there's one last ticket,
if you wanna see the show

And I watched Ol' Massaw walkin'
out of the Gaderenes
With the pigs and all the legions
down into the smithereens

Sons of darkness, Sons of Light,
down to the last hard man
Angels in among them
with savage weapons in their hands

Pale horse walkin' down
way down to the killin' ground
Way down yonder
where there ain't no sound

Out past Nod
where there's nothin' but tears
I ain't gonna see you
for at least a thousand years

To the Killin' Ground

Give me water, give me wine,
Give me vinegar when it's time
Walkin' to Golgotha to pay for my crimes
Walkin' to the killin' ground

Give me loaves and give me fishes
A last supper on holy dishes
Walk me to the garden against my wishes
Walk me to the killin' ground

Gonna lay down my sword
Gonna lay down my shield
And pick em up again on the killin' fields
A shining spear I'm gonna wield
Down in the killin' ground

Raise up my dusty bones
From my bed of carnal stone
Like Lazarus walkin' home
From the killin' ground

There is no sorrow He can't ease
Like Wind thru the olive trees
His mercies will appease me
In the killin' ground

cj fletcher

About the Author

cj fletcher is a composite of a lifetime of influences ranging from World Religions to Urban Legends. A World traveler, he's been a soldier, a counterintelligence agent, a security specialist, a singing cowboy, poet, songwriter, and guitarist.

The songs contained in this book are real. They may be purchased at most digital music outlets. The albums are *ghost town* and *Ocean Boy*, both by cj fletcher.

The music, poetry, and stories by cj fletcher are rife with clues, mysteries, and secrets. He invites you to unravel them.

If you dare.

cj fletcher

Previous Works

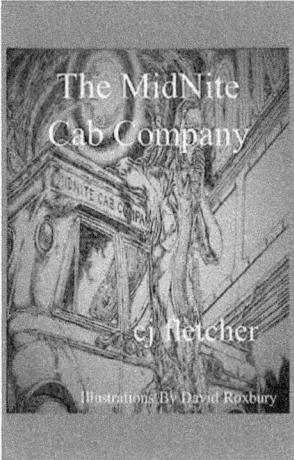

The MidNite Cab Company (2022) – A collection of 24 short stories of flash fiction.

The "MidNite Cab Company" never existed, yet, it is always present. "Driver 51" never was, but, always is. The dilemmas faced by both are not 100% true, yet, they are also faced by many of us on a daily basis. Driver 51 was never a hero, never a savior, yet he bears witness to the twists and turns of the events portrayed in this volume. The best lies contain a kernal of truth, and the truth many times begins from a lie. Throw caution to the wind, step into the rabbit hole, and decide for yourself.

Available on Amazon at: https://www.amazon.com/dp/B0BKRZX3VF